LINTBALL LEO'S

not-so- stupid

Questions

about your

Body

LINTBALL LEO'S

not-so- stupid

Questions

about your Body

Dr. Walt LARIMORE

with John RIDDLE

Illustrations by
Mike Phillips

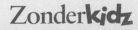
Zonderkidz

Zonder**kidz**®

The children's group of Zondervan

www.zonderkidz.com

Lintball Leo's Not-So-Stupid Questions About Your Body

Copyright © 2003 by Walt Larimore

Requests for information should be addressed to:

Zondervan: Grand Rapids, Michigan 49530

ISBN: 0310705452

Written by: Walt Larimore with John Riddle

Editor: Gwen Ellis

Design: Tobias' Outerwear For Books

Art Direction: Jody Langley

Production Artist: Merit Alderink

 [CIP pending]

Printed in U.S.A.

06 07 08 09 /❖DC/ 9 8 7 6 5 4

To Scott, who taught me so very much about being a dad.
–Walt

For Hunter and Mikey and Charlie,
and all the other boys who are looking for answers.
–M.P.

Contents

What is  SOUL GEAR **?**

Based on Luke 2:52:
"And Jesus grew in wisdom and stature,
and in favor with God and men (NIV)."

2:52 is designed just for boys 8-12!
This verse is one of the only verses in
the Bible that provides a glimpse of Jesus
as a young boy. Who doesn't wonder what
Jesus was like as a kid?

Become smarter, stronger, deeper,
and cooler as you develop
into a young man of God
with 2:52 Soul Gear™!

The 2:52 Soul Gear™ takes a closer look by focusing on the four major areas of development highlighted in Luke 2:52:

"Wisdom" = mental/emotional = **Smarter**

"Stature" = physical = **Stronger**

"Favor with God" = spiritual = **Deeper**

"Favor with man" = social = **Cooler**

Chapter 1

The Good, the Bad, and the Ugly?

"Ouch! That hurts," cried a tiny, mysterious voice from the piece of bellybutton lint Steve held between his fingers. "You want a piece of me? I'm not afraid of you!"

Steve hurried to his desk and picked up the magnifying glass he used to examine bugs. He looked carefully at the talking piece of lint that was now yelling like a squashed cat. Steve released his pinching

grip and the piece of lint brushed himself off, fixed his hair, and fluffed out the finger squeeze marks from his stomach.

Hey!!

You want a piece of me!?!

"Who are you?" asked Steve.

"I'm Lintball Leo, at your service," Leo answered taking a bow.

"Wow, a talking piece of lint. I must be dreaming," said Steve.

"This is no dream. Here. I'll pinch you." Leo tried to pinch Steve's hand, but his fingers were so small that Steve didn't feel a thing."

"Did you feel that?" asked Leo.

Not wanting to be impolite, Steve said, "That was some pinch. I guess I'm not dreaming after all."

Leo flexed his muscles. "I work out and eat only good, nutritious stuff. Gotta stay strong, you know."

"How long have you been living in my belly button?" Steve asked.

"Oh, I've been around for a few years now. Sometimes when you tried to clean your belly-button, you knocked me down to other parts of your body," Leo told Steve. "I visited your feet once, and while it was nice to see my relatives who live down between your toes, I think I'd rather live in your bellybutton."

"Uh . . . I have things living between my toes?" asked Steve, looking a little nervous.

Relax!   You're not going to turn into a big hairy monster...   ...overnight!

"Relax, Steve. It's no big deal. All guys have a little extra dirt here and there. Hey! I've been most everywhere on your body, and I'm becoming an expert in boy-body anatomy. I'll be hanging around until you reach puberty. Then you won't need me anymore and I'll find another boy's bellybutton to call home."

"Puberty," said Steve. "I've heard that word

"Jesus grew in...stature, and in favor with God and men."
Luke 2:52

before. Can you tell me what it means?"

"No problem." Leo drew himself up to his full fluffy height. "Puberty sounds like a strange word, but it's something that happens to all people. Puberty happens when young bodies start to change and mature—from boys into men, from girls into women.

Puberty?

Steve had a look of horror on his face.

"What's with the face? Don't panic! Puberty doesn't mean you're going to start shaving next week. It just means that most people begin to change into adults somewhere between the ages of nine and fifteen. And it doesn't happen all at once. Puberty can last anywhere from two to four years."

"That long?" asked Steve.

"Ah, it goes fast. Especially when you start thinking about *girls*."

Steve blushed bright red.

"Puberty can be a pretty confusing time," Leo said. "But it helps if you remember it's all part of growing up. God made your body and this is the way he wants it to work—so

BEFORE.

AFTER.

don't sweat it."

"What if I don't *want* to go through puberty?" asks Steve.

"Unfortunately, that's not an option," Leo sighed. "When the time is right for you, it will just happen.

Then, you'll become a man. That's the good news."

"How old are you?" Steve tried to get a better look at Leo. Are you older than dirt?"

"Very funny, Steve. Let me give you some advice. I've been here and there over the years, and I've seen the good, the bad, and the ugly."

"*Now* you're talking about girls." Steve joked.

"Hey, another funny one. No, I'm not talking about girls. I'm talking about boys and how puberty affects them."

Steve looked worried. "Will this puberty thing hurt? I mean should I wear a helmet?"

With that Lintball Leo rolled up into a ball and

Get Smarter

Growing up isn't easy to do. It would be less complicated if there were a training manual telling you what to expect throughout puberty. But we don't have a manual, and even if we did, everybody grows at a different pace and in a different way. Get smart by finding an older male you can talk to. The best person would be your dad. If he's not available, consider a youth pastor or counselor at your school. Ask very specific questions about growing up. Listen carefully to the answers. Then ask God to help you.

began laughing hysterically. "A helmet! That's very funny! Ha ha ha ..."

"Uh, Mr. Leo, when you get through laughing, do

you think I could ask you some questions about my body?" Steve asked. "I've been too embarrassed to ask my parents or teachers. What do you say? Could you help me out?"

"Why certainly," said Lintball Leo. "But you'll have to promise that you'll stop calling me Mr. Leo. (Whispering.) *That makes me sound so old.* Please, just call me Lintball."

"OK, Lintball, I'll do that," Steve said with a smile.

"So shoot, Steve? You can ask me anything."

2

I'm Not Liking My Body

"Yum, yum, this grape tastes great!" Leo said, as he wiped grape juice from his chin. "You like grapes, Steve?"

Steve thought for a moment and answered. "Yeah, I guess so. Grapes are okay, but my favorite fruit is the banana," he said.

Lintball Leo started laughing again. "Ha, ha, that's 'ripe,'" he said.

Steve looked puzzled. "Hey, what's so funny about a banana?"

Leo stopped laughing and answered. "Well a banana comes in

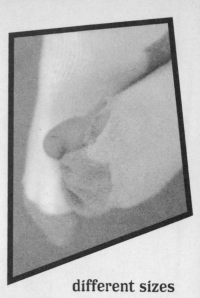

different sizes and changes colors faster than most boys change their socks."

Steve thought about that for a moment and agreed. "Yeah, you're right. When my mom brings bananas home from the supermarket, they're usually green. But within a few days, they change colors—and sometimes I'm still wearing the same pair of socks!" Steve laughed and then got serious.

"Hey Lintball, when you think about it, bananas

In all the world, there is no one else who is exactly like you!

are lucky," he said.

Lintball Leo looked puzzled and asked, "How do you figure?"

Steve thought for a moment before answering. "Well, they get to change their looks from a green skin to a yellow skin. And when they change, people like them better," he said.

"Of course, then they end up being eaten," Lintball answered.

"I praise you because I am wonderfully made."
Psalm 139:14

"Good point," said Steve. "But sometimes I don't like my body, and I wish I could change it."

"Your concerns are perfectly normal, Steve. Most young boys have times when they don't like their bodies," Lintball told him.

"Yeah, I suppose," Steve didn't sound convinced.

Lintball continued. "Remember, Steve, that God designed boys to become men—to be masculine. So it's normal to be concerned about your body and how it looks. There are times when growing from a boy into a man can be embarrassing with so many physical changes beginning to take place."

"Yeah. I know I have to change or stay a kid forever. But sometimes I just look in the mirror and get disgusted with what I see," said Steve.

Lintball Leo gave Steve a reassuring pat on his thumb. "Steve, part of becoming a real man is learning to trust that God is in control and his ways are better than your ways. It's perfectly normal to wonder if God knows what he's doing. Just remember that the Bible says God designed you even while you were still in your mother's womb (Psalm 139:13). He has made you to be com-pletely unique. No one in the history of mankind will have your fingerprints or your DNA or even your personality."

Steve smiled a little. He began to feel better about himself.

Lintball continued, "All boys experience physical changes in their bodies at different times. There is no right or wrong when it comes to the speed and order of those changes. With some boys, hair starts to grow under their arms first while for other boys it starts first on their legs. It happens early for some boys and later for others. God has designed the perfect system for each boy."

Steve asked, "Lintball, I keep seeing ads on TV and in magazines for vitamins, protein drinks, and something called 'supplements.' Will they help my body grow faster?"

"No, Steve," Leo answered. "There's not much you can do to accelerate your growth and development. God has designed you the way you are, and those things will do almost nothing to speed the process along. The best thing you can do for your body is to eat a balanced diet and exercise every day. That will help you grow strong."

"A balanced diet?" Steve giggled. "Does that mean I have to balance my food on my plate before I can eat it?"

Lintball Leo started laughing again. "Hey, Steve, you sure are a funny boy! I can just see you now, trying to balance your peas and carrots on top of your mashed potatoes on a plate on top of your head!"

Then Steve asked Leo a serious question. "My friend Ralph's voice is sounding really weird these days. Sometimes when the teacher calls on him in class, he sounds like he's making his voice go higher and lower when he answers. He says it doesn't bother him, but I think he's really starting

Get Cooler

The Bible says we are fearfully and wonderfully made. When you look at your body, do you get the "fearfully made" part and wonder about the "wonderfully made" part? (Psalm 139:14) It's cool to be realistic about your body. God didn't make junk. He made you the way he wanted you to be. You may not like what you see, but he designed you the way you are. The rest of that verse says, "your works are wonderful, I know that full well." Take a good look in the mirror and try to see what God sees—something unique and special and wonderful.

to worry about it. Will that happen to me?"

"I don't know. During puberty not every boy's voice will crack when he speaks or sings. But yes, your voice will begin to deepen, sooner or later. That, too, is part of the growing-up process, and you shouldn't worry about it." Lintball Leo stood up and began to stretch. "Boy, I'm stuffed after eating that grape. I need some exercise. Hold your hand still while I run a few laps. Got to take my own advice. Got to stay in shape, you know." Leo began

jogging around Steve's hand, and after a minute,

plopped down and took a little rest.

"Boy, that was some workout!" Leo exclaimed.

"I'm beat. Excuse me while I take a quick nap . . .

ZZZZZZZ . . . ZZZZZZZ . . ."

What You Can Expect

10 Years Old

Your male hormones — especially testosterone — are just beginning to become really active, even though there are few bodily signs just yet. Your body is preparing for a series of rapid changes over the next few years.

11 Years and 6 Months

Your scrotum is beginning to enlarge, but your penis isn't changing yet.

12 Years Old

You may experience a painful swelling under one or both breasts. This happens to about one in three boys. It's temporary. Don't worry; you're not growing breasts! But if it persists, be sure your doctor takes a look.

12 Years and 6 Months

You are beginning to grow taller faster. Your chest wall is becoming wider and deeper. Fine, soft hair (pubic hair) is beginning to show up at the base of your penis. The frequency of erections (your penis getting hard) increases dramatically.

13 Years and 6 Months

Your voice begins to deepen and may crack while singing or speaking. Your pubic hair starts to darken and become thicker and longer. Your scrotum and testicles are growing more rapidly. The skin on your penis may begin to get darker. Also, your penis is now beginning to lengthen, but does not yet get bigger around. "Wet dreams" may occur. These dreams, usually involving members of the opposite sex, can cause some of the sperm or fluid from the testicles (called "the ejaculate") to come out of your penis and dampen your pajamas or shorts.

14 Years Old

Your pubic hair continues to thicken and covers a larger area. Your penis begins to grow — both in length and width.

14 yrs. 6 mos.

Your growth speeds up. Doctors call this a "growth spurt"! Hair growth begins in your armpits. Your sweat glands produce more sweat, and it develops a distinctive odor (called "body odor" or "BO"). Pimples (early acne — whiteheads and blackheads) may form on your face. Your face and body look more and more like that of a young adult.

15 Years Old

Facial hair growth begins on your chin and upper lip. Your skin can get more oily and acne can worsen. Your voice gets deeper, and you begin to sound more like an adult.

- -

16 Years Old

Your pubic hair growth and distribution and your penis size is similar to more mature men. Your facial hair is thicker and spreads across more of your face. Many young men begin shaving at about this age. Hair growth on your legs begins to increase. You are nearing your full adult height.

- -

18 Years Old

Your body shape is mature.

- -

20-22 Years Old

Complete sexual maturity. Body hair is more distributed.

" Anyone who
enters God's
rest also
rests from his
own work."
Hebrews 4:8

Chapter 3

Getting My Zzzzzzs

Zzzzzzzzzzzzz . . . Lintball was still snoring away.

Steve just stood there holding out his hand and

waiting patiently for his new friend to awaken.

Finally, Lintball Leo opened one eye, stretched,

and yawned. "Ah,

that was great!"

he exclaimed.

"There's nothing

like a quick cat-

nap to keep a

You need about 9 to 9 1/2 hours of sleep every night.

piece of lint looking his best."

Steve asked, "Hey Lintball, you live by yourself, don't you? I mean, there aren't other things living in my bellybutton that I can't see, are there?"

Lintball laughed, "I sure do. Just how much room do you think there is in your bellybutton, anyway?" He started stretching his arms as he continued to wake up. "Why do you ask? Did you think I had a

"Let us, therefore, make every effort to enter that rest." Hebrews 4:10

whole army of lintballs living there with me?"

Steve thought about how gross *that* would be. "Uh, no, I was just asking because it must be nice to live alone and not have parents telling you what to do all of the time."

"Oh, yes, parents," Leo sighed. "You can't live with 'em and you can't live without 'em, I always say."

Steve nodded his head.

"Lintball, when you were living with your parents, were they always telling you to get more sleep? It seems like that's all my parents tell me these days. *You need more sleep!* Over and over again they tell me that. It's enough to drive me nuts!"

"Well, Steve, let *me* ask you," Leo responded. "Are you getting enough sleep? I mean, if your parents are concerned, there must be some reason."

"Like what?" Steve asked.

"Well, for example, do you ever find yourself falling asleep 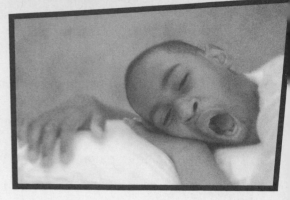 during classes at school? Do you come home from school and want to take a nap instead of going out to play? If so, then your parents are probably right. You're probably not getting enough sleep."

Steve thought for a moment, and then replied. "Some days in school I do get very sleepy in the afternoon. Then I wish I had a pillow with me instead of my book bag," he said.

"Hey, now there's an idea!" Lintball Leo said as he snapped his fingers. "A book bag that is also a pillow. Great idea, Steve!"

Lintball started walking in circles, as he got more excited about the idea. "Think about the possibilities! Yoo hoo! I am a marketing genius!" Leo exclaimed.

"What in the world are you so excited about?" asked Steve.

"A back pack that can be used as a pillow! Just think how many students would be able to take naps at their desks?" Then as Lintball Leo began to think about an entire room filled with students sleeping at their desks, he realized that wouldn't work at all. "Well, come to think of it, I guess teachers wouldn't like that kind of a book bag too much, would they?"

"No, I guess not, but it is a pretty cool idea," Steve said. "Now let's get serious. Just how much sleep do I really need? It seems like I have so many things to do—after-school activities, homework, church, sports, and there are so many good TV programs on late at night."

"Hmmm, it sounds like you lead a busy life. Maybe something will have to go so you can get a decent night's sleep. I read an article in the newspaper the other day about kids and sleep.

"You read the newspaper?" Steve asked in amazement.

"I sure do. That's how I get all of my news. You know, I don't have a TV. The reception in your belly button would be terrible!" he said.

"Anyway, this article said medical studies show more and more teens are staying up late and then falling asleep in class. Some teens even arrive late for their classes because they oversleep! It's an epidemic of tiredness."

Lintball continued, "But seriously, Steve, you should make sure you get enough sleep each night. Medical researchers have shown that the average teen needs nine to nine-and-a-half hours of sleep each night.

Steve's mouth dropped open. "Nine-and-a-half hours? If I did that, I'd be spending all my free time in bed."

"It might seem that way," Leo said, "But just think how great you'll feel when you're awake. If you get less than nine hours, your athletic performance could begin to drop off. And some researchers think that lack of sleep contributes to depression in teens."

Steve listened to what Lintball Leo was saying.

"Did you know that a lack of sleep could also affect your grades?" Lintball went on, "Teens who get the most sleep tend to get As and Bs. So just remember that restful sleep energizes you and allows your body and mind to recover from the day past and prepare for the next."

"Now you sound like my parents."

"Well, Steve, I remember you asking me about what you could do to grow strong. Did you know that restful sleep releases a growth hormone that helps tissues develop properly?

"Huh?" Steve's face showed his surprise.

"Yep, sleep helps form the red blood cells that deliver oxygen to your body and brain. Sleep also promotes healthy bone growth."

"You know an awful lot for a piece of lint," said Steve.

Leo grinned because he knew he had made his point with Steve.

"I'll take that as a compliment," said Leo.

"Sounds like I'd better start going to bed earlier than I have been, Leo," Steve said. "But sometimes I have trouble falling asleep when I go to bed."

"You can help yourself with that. Before bedtime, try to unwind from the day by reading a book or your Bible, writing about your day in a journal, or just listening to soothing music."

"Yes, those are good ideas," said Steve.

"What you don't want to do is play exciting video games, listen to noisy rock music, or watch some

Get Stronger

Most guys want to grow up to be physically strong. That's a good thing. But they use some pretty scary things to grow stronger—like steroids, which can be dangerous. Others eat or drink foods that advertisers say will "bulk up your body". Some buy expensive exercise equipment. But one of the best ways to build a strong body is sleep! Our bodies repair and build themselves when we are asleep, and young people actually grow while they are sleeping. Lots of sleep helps us think and perform better, resist disease, and actually become stronger. So get to bed on time.

violent crime show on TV. Don't think you can drop right off to sleep after that."

"Hmmm. That's what I've been doing. OK. I'll give your way a try before I go to bed tonight."

"So, how can you get the proper amount of sleep?" Leo continued. "Here are just a few tips that are recommended by experts."

- Don't eat or drink foods or beverages with caffeine, such as soft drinks, coffee, and chocolate after 4:00 P.M.

- Don't watch exciting, thrilling, violent, or scary TV shows or movies right before bed time.

- Don't read books that might keep you from falling asleep.

- Don't nap excessively during the day. More than thirty minutes may keep you from falling asleep later. And, recent studies show that a ten-minute "power nap" will give you the most energy and will not prevent you from falling asleep at bedtime.

- Don't wait until the night before a big test to study. Staying up all night can mess up your sleep patterns and your performance on the test. Plan to do your studies way ahead of time.

- Don't use a computer for the last hour or so before bedtime. The light from the computer monitor signals to your brain that it's time to wake up. The same thing can be true for the TV.

- Do exercise regularly. It will improve your sleep. But exercising right before bedtime can make falling asleep more difficult.

- Do try to go to bed and wake up at the same time every day (or at least most of the days of the week).

• Do get into bright light in the morning—it will wake you up and get you going.

• Before bedtime, try to unwind from the day. You can do this by meditating, reading your Bible or a peaceful book, journaling, or listening to soothing music.

• Do try to stick with your regular sleep schedule on weekends. You can't catch up on missed sleep from the week before.

Chapter 4

I'm so mad I could...

"Ah, feathers!" said Lintball Leo.

"What did you say?" asked Steve, sounding puzzled.

"I said 'Ah, feathers.'"

Steve laughed. "What does that mean?"

"It means I got mad because I'm always getting hung up on something," said Lintball Leo, as he tried to untangle himself from some tape.

Steve chuckled.

"What's so funny about getting stuck?" asked Lintball.

Steve laughed harder. "Nothing's funny about you getting stuck on tape. What I was really laughing at was what you said–'Ah feathers'."

"Okay, I suppose a talking piece of lint who gets mad when he gets hung up is sort of funny," said Lintball. "But to tell you the truth, a long time ago I would have jumped up and down, shouted, and even said a bad word or two," he admitted to his friend.

"I wasn't always able to control my anger."

"I know about that. Sometimes I get so angry, I just want to yell," Steve said. "Just last week I got so mad at my parents I felt like throwing some-thing.

Lintball Leo tried to smooth down his fuzz where it was stuck together. Then he said, "Now, what was that you were saying about getting angry?"

"My parents," Steve contin-ued. "Sometimes they drive me nuts. Some days it seems as if I can't do any-thing right in their eyes."

"Oh, yes, parents. They say they love you, but then they do things that make you so angry," Lintball agreed.

Steve asked Lintball, "Soooo, what can I do about my getting mad at Mom and Dad?"

Lintball Leo thought for a moment. "Well, let's see. The first thing you need to know is that as you go through puberty, your hormones start firing and there are changes in your brain too. Those two things really contribute to your anger.

"Sometimes you may get angry and afterward you may even feel good about it. That doesn't mean you're turning into some horrible monster."

"Well! That's good to know," said Steve.

"What usually happens when you get angry is that at first you're really angry. But then in a few minutes, you

Getting angry is part of being human.   As long as you learn to cool off.

get over it and begin to feel guilty about your anger."

"Yes, that happens to me!" Steve agreed. "I love my family, but sometimes ..." Steve clenched his fists.

"Well, just be aware that your mood changes can be related to the physical and hormonal changes in your body. There are, however, some things that can help you deal with your anger."

"What can I do, Lintball? Sometimes I feel so helpless. I get angry so quickly."

"In your anger do not sin... trust in the Lord."
Psalm 4:4

"The Bible in Psalms 4:4 teaches that if you get angry, you are not to sin."

"Now, what does that mean?"

"The word that is used means 'don't let your anger break-out'. So it means you are not to do wrong or hurt others when you're angry," Lintball told him. "When you feel that you're about to be angry or you are already angry, the first step is to recognize it. Admit your anger to yourself and God. Then, you need to learn effective ways to deal with anger."

"I can do that if you tell me how," Steve said.

"Good," Lintball replied. "One approach is to learn how to 'cool down.' When something gets you really ticked off, take a time-out. Stop, calm down, and think before you do or say anything. You can take a walk or go to your room for some quiet time. You might need to pray or listen to some calming music or write in your journal about how you are feeling."

"You've mentioned a journal a couple of times. I think I better start keeping a journal today," Steve said.

"That's a great idea. Putting your feelings down on paper is a great way to get the anger on the outside. Another good way to work off steam is to go outside and run or kick a ball around. Or maybe you can find a friend to talk with about your anger. Everyone deals with anger in a different way, but the best way is to deal with it on a positive note. Don't let the anger take control of you," said Lintball.

"Hey, Lintball, those sound like really good ideas. Thanks, little buddy. The next time I feel angry, I'm going to try some of them."

"You're welcome, big buddy," Lintball replied. "Remember that it's always better to talk about

a problem you are having, instead of reacting to it. And guess what, your parents went through the same feelings and events when they were growing up."

Steve nodded his head. "Yeah, I guess when my parents were young, they probably got mad at their parents too."

"One more thing to remember, Steve," Lintball continued. "Once you've cooled down a bit, spend some time thinking about what caused your anger. Try to figure out why it affected you so much. Then, use some of the wisdom that the Lord has given you. Try to think of some solutions and what the consequences of those solutions might be."

"Sounds like a better way to deal with anger than the way I've been doing it," said Steve. "But I do have one more question, if you don't mind my asking."

"Not at all," Lintball Leo replied. "Ask away."

"Why do you say 'Ah, feathers,' when you get mad?" Steve asked.

"Oh, that's easy," Lintball replied. "When I was a little piece of lint, my parents would send me to my

Get Deeper

I'm so mad I could..." Have you ever said that? Most everyone has. When going through puberty you may feel angry and not even know why. You may feel restless and just want to hit something. That's because your hormones may be kicking in and are somewhat out of control. It's a tough time for you and everyone around you. This is a great time to ask for God's help in controlling your anger. He has promised to hear us when we pray and ask for help.

room when I got angry. I spent so much time on my pillow that all I could think of was, 'Ah, feathers,'" Lintball said.

At that Steve gave Lintball a high five.

Tattoos and Stuff: Do You Really Want to Take the Risk?

"Hey Lintball, can I ask you a personal question?"

Steve asked his friend.

Lintball Leo replied, "Sure, ask away. What is your 'personal' question about? Girls? I'm quite the 'ladies man,' you know."

"No, it's not about girls right now, although I do have a few questions for later," Steve said. "My question is about body piercing. A lot of my friends are getting their bodies pierced. They think it makes them look cool. I think they just look weird. My personal question is this: Have you ever had part of your body pierced?"

At that Lintball Leo started laughing. "Oh, that's funny. Can you imagine a piece of lint getting a body piercing? Ha, ha, ha, please, you're killing me!"

Lintball rolled back and forth across Steve's hand and held his sides.

"Hey, that tickles," said Steve, who joined in the laughter with his friend.

Lintball composed himself a few seconds later. "Sorry about that, Steve. Sometimes I get carried away and howl with laughter! Just the thought of me with my tongue or my navel pierced is funny—to say the least."

"But so many kids I know are getting a body piercing. So if that many people are doing it, it must be all right, don't you think?" Steve asked.

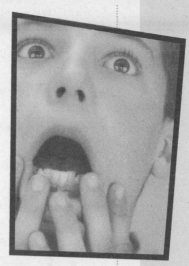

"Oh Steve, just because a lot of people do something doesn't mean it's safe or the best thing to do," replied Lintball. "If all of your friends decided to jump off a bridge, you wouldn't follow them, would you?"

"No, of course not! You sound like my mother. She always says that." But Steve was thinking hard about what his linty friend had said.

"People don't know how dangerous body piercing can be," said Lintball Leo.

"Really? It's dangerous?" Steve was surprised.

"Yes. Body piercing has become very popular. Shops have opened up practically everywhere, and there is little or no regulation. Here's the scary part. When there are no rules or health regulations to follow, infections and other health hazards can happen."

"Wow! I never thought about it being unhealthy," said Steve.

"Well, you should. Body piercing can cause infection, scarring, and tetanus, which can be fatal," said Lintball Leo. "Some heavy-duty professional health organizations are against all forms of body piercing, with just one exception. Guess what that is."

Steve thought about it for a moment. "I know, it's the ear lobe, right?"

"We have a winner!" Lintball Leo was jumping up and down. "Give that boy a bag of potato chips."

"But why is it safe to get your ear lobes pieced?" Steve asked.

"Because unlike the other areas of the body that kids like to get pierced, the ear lobe is made of

fatty tissue and has a great blood supply. Those are factors known to protect you in the event of an infection. And most shops that pierce ears use piercing guns that are sterile.

"Oh, okay," Steve said. Lintball scrunched up his forehead. "But I have a question too. Why does any-one need to be pierced?"

Steve seemed to be deep in thought for a moment,

"God's temple is sacred, and you are that temple."
1 Corinthians 3:16

then said, "Okay, I'm convinced piercing is not the best thing to do, but hey, Lintball, how about a tattoo? Is it all right to get a tattoo?"

Lintball Leo screamed "No way!" Steve jumped at that and jerked his hand, which caused Lintball to fall over backward. "Sorry," he said as he stood up once again. "I get carried away when I hear about young people wanting to get a tattoo," he said.

"Oh no, not me," Steve said. "I'm not thinking about getting a tattoo—I hate needles!"

How about maybe a pretty little flamingo?

"Well, don't ever get a tattoo. First of all, tattooing is a very painful process and if you ever change your mind after having one—too bad! It will be expensive and painful to remove, and you're likely to end up with ugly scars," said Lintball.

Lintball continued. "Worse yet, there are health

risks when you get a tattoo. In most states tattoo parlors are not regulated. So the people doing the tattoos can use unclean equipment, ink, or needles. They can infect you with a life-long, incurable infections, such as hepatitis, or even HIV/AIDS. And if you don't think this risk is real, think again. It is such a big risk that the American Association of Blood Banks won't accept blood donations until one year after a person has gotten a tattoo. They want to give the infection time to show up before they take your blood," said Lintball Leo.

"Getting a tattoo doesn't sound like a smart thing to do either," said Steve.

Get Smarter

Do you know anyone who wants to get a tattoo or a body piercing? Do you know someone who already has one? Before you think about doing either one, be sure you read this chapter and learn about the dangers involved. And be sure to talk with your parents. There are many good reasons not to pierce your body or get a tattoo. Remember these markings are permanent—especially tattoos. You may not want a tattoo in 20 years, but if you have one, you are stuck with it for the rest of your life. You really need to think ahead on this one. You need to get smart about it.

"You're absolutely right. And I read that some of the dyes used in tattooing are not even approved for use in humans!" Lintball exclaimed.

Steve just shook his head. "Piercing and tattoos are not for me!"

"Yes, I knew you were too smart to consider doing either one," Lintball replied. "I had an Uncle who once thought about getting a tattoo. But he was smart; and before he went ahead with it, he talked to a few other lintballs who had gotten tattoos. He learned that as they grew older, they regretted their decision."

"Your uncle was one smart piece of lint," said Steve.

"Yep, he was. Let's hope that other boys and other lintballs are as smart as my uncle!" replied Lintball.

Chapter

6

Hair: Up Here, and Down There

"Hey Lintball, do you shave everyday?" Steve

asked. Lintball Leo looked at his young friend to

see if this was a trick question. "Are

you making fun of me, Steve?

Think about it for a minute.

Why would a piece of lint

have to shave?"

"Oh, good point," Steve

replied. "I was just

63

curious. I see my father and my older brother shaving, and I just wondered when I will need to start shaving too."

"Well don't rush it, sport. I hear men complain all

the time about having to shave daily. Most young guys think it's really cool when they first start shaving, but after a while, it becomes 'just another chore' on their 'to do' list," said Lintball Leo.

"Wow, I never thought about that. I always thought it would be cool to get to shave. But now that you mention it, I suppose shaving in the morning while I'm getting ready for school could get old," said Steve. "But how will I know when it's time for me to start shaving? Will I get an e-mail saying 'Hey, today's the day!'" he asked.

"An e-mail—what a cute idea," Lintball replied. "I can just see God sitting at his computer late at night getting ready to send e-mails to all the young men who need to start shaving in the morning."

"Yeah, that does sound kind of silly," Steve said.

"Once again, every boy develops at a different pace," Lintball Leo said. "Some young men start shaving when they're 12 or 13, while others

Remember the
"Little Engine
That Could"?

don't start until they're 17 or 18. You'll first start

noticing what's called 'peach fuzz' on your face. It's

barely noticeable, but that will be the arrival of

your facial hair. The important thing is not to

worry about whether you are developing too fast or

too slow."

"Will I be able to grow a mustache or sideburns

right away?" Steve asked enthusiastically.

"But grow in
the grace and
knowledge of
our Lord and
Savior Jesus
Christ."
2 Peter 3:18

"You really won't know until your facial hair starts coming in," replied Lintball Leo. "Some boys will be able to grow sideburns, while others will only have patches of facial hair coming in here and there."

Steve looked startled. "You mean, my face could look like I have crop circles?"

Lintball started laughing hysterically once again. "Ha, ha, ha," he said. "Steve, you have a great future as a stand-up comic! Ha, ha, ha."

Steve was proud that Lintball thought he was funny. "So, you really think I say funny things?" Steve asked.

"You sure do, my boy, you sure do," said Lintball Leo, as he stood up and composed himself once again.

"Hey Lintball, while we're on the subject of body hair, what can you tell me about pubic... you know... hair... down there?" Steve asked.

"Pubic hair? What would you like to know, Steve? Anything in particular that you're curious about?" Lintball Leo asked.

"Well, to tell you the truth, I'm the only one in my gym class without any. Am I doing something wrong or are you going to tell me again that everybody grows it at a different rate?" Steve asked.

"I'm going to tell you that you are perfectly normal. Yes, all boys mature and develop at different ages, and that can be painfully obvious when you shower with others after a gym class or a sports event."

"Tell me about it," Steve said. "But so far no one is teasing me."

"That's great because it's not any fun to be teased, especially about your lack of pubic hair," Lintball Leo said. "Just don't worry about when it will start growing. On average by 12-1/2 years of age, most young men have fine, soft pubic hair that begins to show up at the base of the penis. By 13-1/2 years of age the pubic hair begins to darken and become

Get Stronger

One of the surest signs that a boy is growing into a man is when hair begins to appear on his face. It's also growing elsewhere on his body. Some boys think it's cool and some are really embarrassed. Some boys don't get facial hair as soon as others and they begin to wonder if they are normal. They are. God has a design and a purpose for each boy and a plan for when he will fully become a man—and it is not the same plan for every boy. If you can, just relax and enjoy where you are in God's plan right now. You'll be shaving every day before you know it.

thicker and longer. Usually by the time a boy is 14 years old, his pubic hair is longer and more coarse and covers a larger area."

"Thanks for the info, Lintball," said Steve. "You sure have a way of making a boy feel secure."

Chapter 7

What's That Smell and What Are Those Zits Doing Here?

"Hey Steve," Lintball Leo asks, "how often do you take a shower?" Steve was surprised by the question, and started to smell under his armpits. "Why, do I stink or something?" he asked defensively.

"No, you don't stink. In

fact, you're one of the cleanest boys I have lived on in a long time," Lintball Leo replied.

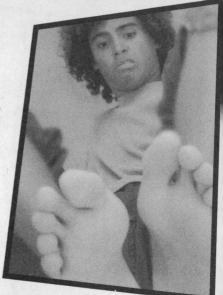

"You've lived on other boys?" Steve's eyes grew huge.

"Yep, I have. You know, Steve, that as you get older, and that puberty

thing starts to kick in, you will start to notice a

new smell coming from under

your arms and other parts of

your body. It's what I call the

P-U in puberty," he said, as

he held his nose.

"Yeah, I know what you

mean," Steve replied. "Some

of my friends are starting to

stink. Is that normal? Is

there a cure? Should I start

stocking up on deodorant?"

"Yes, it's normal for boys to start producing body

odor, better known as BO, when they start going

through puberty. That's because during puberty

their sweat glands produce more sweat than

before. Did you know you can also have body odor

from your feet," said Lintball Leo.

"From my feet?" Steve asked in disbelief. "Did

your relatives down there tell you that?"

"No, they didn't need to because *most* boys have smelly feet," Lintball Leo replied. "That's why it's important to wash your feet thoroughly and change your socks everyday. And if you wear tennis shoes, you should make sure you wear cotton athletic socks. They help keep your feet dry by absorbing the sweat that your feet produce."

"Yuck, sweaty feet," Steve said while holding his nose and looking down at his feet.

"You can help reduce the offensive body odor by taking a shower or bath everyday," Lintball Leo advised. "Washing with soap and using a deodorant will get rid of most strong body odors. Sometimes it helps to put a little foot powder in your shoes."

If God asks you to do something... ...He will give you the strength and the power... ...to do it!

"It's not easy going through this puberty thing, is it, Lintball?" Steve asked his little fuzzy friend.

"No, it's not real easy. Some boys sweat a lot, while other boys only sweat a little," Lintball Leo said. "So those boys who sweat a lot probably feel like puberty is harder on them than on boys who only sweat a little. You'll probably sweat about the same amount as your father did when he was going

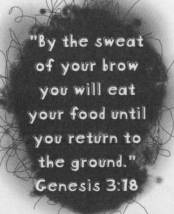

"By the sweat of your brow you will eat your food until you return to the ground." Genesis 3:18

through puberty. You could always ask him about it, you know," Lintball Leo advised.

"Yeah, I suppose I could ask my Dad ," Steve said thoughtfully. "But it's much more fun talking to you, Lintball Leo."

Lintball took out his small brush, and began brushing his hair and his body. When he was finished, he said, "Now I feel better. My hair was starting to get oily. Has that ever happened to you, Steve?" Lintball Leo asked.

"Well, now that you mention it, I have noticed that my hair is starting to feel oily sometimes. And my face feels oily too. Is that part of the changes my body is going through?" Steve asked his friend.

"You bet. That's why it's important to keep your hair clean—the rest of your body too. Oil also starts to appear on your nose, forehead, and the rest of your face. What happens next is something most young boys dread—*zits* start to appear."

"Oh no," cried Steve. "I thought zits were optional!"

"Ha, ha, ha," Lintball chuckled. "You crack me up! Zits are optional! What an idea!"

Steve started feeling around his face with his free hand. "It doesn't *feel* oily, Lintball," he said. "Maybe I'll only have one or two zits to deal with."

"No one knows, Steve. But don't worry about zits and oily faces," Lintball Leo replied. "If the zits become a big problem, your parents can take you to the doctor. If it's a not-so-big problem, there are wonderful creams and medications at the drugstore to help control them." Lintball Leo fluffed his stomach back into shape and continued. "You just have to make sure you wash your face everyday—sometimes more, especially when you feel it is becoming oily."

"Yeah, I guess I can do that," Steve answered.

"This puberty thing isn't easy, is it, Lintball Leo?"

"No—no one ever said it would be. But the most important thing to remember, Steve, is that God designed you. Your body will mature the way it's supposed to," Lintball Leo said. "It's true that no one likes to have zits or problems with BO or oily skin. But during puberty, your oil and sweat glands are very active. So it becomes a bigger problem than it was before. Having the right attitude helps a lot because when someone sees a smiling, happy face, he or she won't be looking at the zits.

"Yeah, I guess God wouldn't make mistakes. He'd know how to make things the right way," said

Get Cooler

It's not cool to smell bad and have dirty hair. Maybe stink and oil don't bother you, but they will bother people around you. This is a problem that can be fixed quickly. Get in the shower every day, wash your hair, and start using deodorant. Wear clean clothes and put the dirty ones in the hamper so your mother doesn't have to smell your stinky socks. That's a cool way to be considerate of the people you live with.

Steve, "and that includes me. I guess I'll have to learn how to take better care of myself and my body while all of this PU-puberty stuff happens," he said, holding his nose as he picked up his socks.

Chapter 8

Important Stuff About Boy Parts

"I have another personal question." Steve said to

his fuzzy little friend.

"Sure, Steve, ask away. You know you

can ask me anything."

"Well, it's very personal,"

Steve said blushing.

"Now, now, let's not get shy, Steve. If

you have a question that's been bugging

you, please, by all means,

ask it

before it burns a
hole in your head,"
Lintball Leo said.

Steve laughed.
"Hey, that's pretty
funny. You're a funny
piece of lint," he said.
"Anyway, my question is
about my testicles. Sometimes mine itch. Is that
normal? Or is something wrong with me?"

Lintball Leo looked thoughtful for a moment
before answering. "Steve, that's an important question, and I'm glad you asked it. Most boys are probably too afraid to ask a question like that," Lintball
Leo said.

"Well, I kind of need to know," Steve confided.

Leo took a deep breath. "The answer is—yes—it's
completely normal. However, 'normal' itching of
your testicles means it shouldn't happen all

the time."

"Oh, that's good to know," Steve replied with a look of relief. "Sometimes I just want to scratch my testicles, especially when I'm in school. But I know I can't."

"You're right about that!" Lintball replied. "A gentleman never scratches his testicles around other people, especially young women. Scratching of private parts can be very embarrassing to them."

"Yes, I guess that would embarrass them and probably me too," Steve said.

"Now one more thing. You should also know that continuous itching can indicate a problem called 'jock itch,'" said Lintball Leo. "This problem occurs when something called a 'fungal infection' grows on the skin of your scrotum. It can cause itching, redness, and sometimes it can cause your skin to peel

You are not alone.
Everybody feels
the same way
you do.

in the crotch area."

Steve started making faces. "Yuck!"

"Don't worry, Steve," Lintball Leo continued. "It's very common and can be treated with over-the-counter medicated creams."

"Whew!" Steve seemed relieved. Then a thoughtful look crossed his face. "Is that why the doctor needs to touch and feel my testicles during my

"Christ Jesus...being found in appearance as a man humbled himself and became obedient." Philippians 2:8

check-up? Is he looking for jock itch?"

"No, the doctor isn't looking for jock itch," replied Lintball Leo. "When the doctor examines your testicles and the area around them, it's to look for two important things he hopes he won't find—a hernia and a tumor."

Steve looked confused. "What's a hernia and a tumor?" he asked.

"A hernia is a bulge in your groin area caused when the contents of your belly push through a weak spot around your genitals. It's important to have your testicles checked for a hernia when you have your annual physical exam," Lintball Leo said. "It's also vital that the doctor gently check your testicles to be sure there are no cancerous tumors. Although testicular cancer is unusual in young men, it is the second most common cancer seen during the teen years."

"Hey, I remember reading an article about Lance

Armstrong—you know that Tour de France bicycle champion. He had that kind of cancer. Not only did he get well, but he also won the race." Steve exclaimed.

"Yes, he was lucky. His doctor discovered the cancer early enough to save his life," Lintball Leo said. "Your doctor can also show you how to examine your testicles once a month when you shower. But that doesn't mean you should only take one shower a month."

Steve laughed. "Yes, one shower a month doesn't sound like a very good idea. It might lead to that other body problem we talked about—BO!"

"True," Lintball Leo agreed. "The next time you go to the doctor, ask him to show you how to examine yourself. It's really important. Pick a regular day to do your self-examination—like the first day of each month. Then, if you notice any changes at all in your testicles, be sure to let your parents know and have a doctor check you over as soon as possible."

"Good advice, Lintball Leo," Steve said.

"Hey, while we're talking about testicles," Steve said, "my friend says he only has one. Is he telling the truth? And, is that normal?"

"Well, it's not normal, but it's not rare," Lintball Leo replied. "And, the fact that your friend told you this, tells me he has a special trust in you. You must be good friends. So, let me share some facts about boys who have only one testicle."

"I'm all ears," Steve said.

Lintball Leo tried to picture Steve with "all ears." Then he said, "And I'm all fuzz," said Lintball Leo.

Some boys are born with only one testicle. Other boys may lose a testicle—in an accident or because of an infection or because there was some other reason to surgically remove it," Lintball explained.

Steve continued to listen intently.

"But don't ever forget, Steve, that God has designed our bodies very carefully," Lintball Leo continued. "When a boy loses one testicle, the remaining one will do the job of both. It will even grow larger to make up for this extra production. In some cases the doctor will place an artificial testicle in the scrotum so that the appearance of the scrotum is perfectly normal."

"So, it sounds as if any boy who has only one testicle is just as much a man as a guy with two testicles. Right?" Steve asked his fuzzy friend.

"You're absolutely right!" Lintball Leo agreed.

Chapter 9

The "M" Word

Steve looked a little uncomfortable, and Lintball Leo had the feeling he still had questions. "Well, now, Steve, what's on your mind?" asked Lintball Leo.

Steve looked down and whispered, "It's masturbation."

"Oh, Steve!" exclaimed Lintball,

"don't be embar-
rassed. I don't mind
talking about that
subject at all."

"Are you sure?"

"Not at all," Lintball
Leo answered. "Asking
questions and talking
with someone who knows about your body helps
you get information that is accurate and correct.
And masturbation is something every normal young
man is interested in."

Steve looked more at ease.

"And, it's also helpful to know that just about all
boys have masturbated," Lintball Leo explained.
"So to set the record straight, a lot of the information that gets passed around is not true.
Masturbation is not harmful to your body. It does
not cause blindness, weakness, mental retardation,
or any other physical problem. Another myth is
that if you masturbate you'll run out of sperm and
not be able to have children. That's just not true!

But masturbation can have emotional and spiritual effects."

"Oh? How's that?" asked Steve.

"Well, one effect is that a young man can experience guilt and feel real bad after he masturbates. This can lead to psychological and spiritual harm. Another potential effect of masturbation is that some boys will masturbate over and over until it becomes an addiction they can't control."

"Wow, that's serious!" Steve said.

"It can be very serious!" Lintball Leo replied. "Steve, anything that begins to dominate your thinking or actions is not likely to be pleasing to the Lord."

Steve furrowed his brow. "Lintball, does the Bible talk about masturbation?"

"Well, the Bible never specifically mentions

masturbation, but it talks a lot about being sexually pure and about pure thinking. Paul told a very young Timothy, 'Don't let anyone look down on you because you are young, but set an example for the believers in speech, in life, in love, in faith and in purity'."

"So, are you saying masturbation is impure—or, a sin?"

"Well, the Bible doesn't tell us, Steve. But, it's important to understand that masturbation is usu-

ally accompanied by sexual thoughts or images. Because of this, many pastors and Bible teachers believe it is always wrong."

"God has given sex to us to be used only in marriage," Lintball went on. "So, if you're putting images in your mind that are sexual—like sexually explicit TV shows, videos, or magazines—or, if you're thinking wrongly about girls at school—well, that's what the Bible calls lust. And the Bible is clear that we are to flee or run from lust and sexual immorality."

"But, I don't know if I can do that Lintball!" Steve cried out.

"You can choose the kind of thoughts you dwell on. Boys who choose not to dwell on impure thoughts may find it easier not to masturbate, not because masturbation is bad or a sin, but because these boys don't want the impure thoughts they have while they are masturbating."

"How are these thoughts harmful?" asked Steve—almost bewildered.

"Emotionally they can affect your marriage later on because a boy's brain is designed to be stimulated by sexual images. Boys remember for a

" Create in me a pure heart, O God, and renew a steadfast spirit within me."
Psalm 51:10

long, long time any sexual images they see. Steve, let me see if I can prove this to you by asking you a very personal question. OK?"

"OK."

"Have you seen a picture of a girl or a woman who is not dressed?"

Steve blushed. "Actually, I've seen some that other boys brought to school."

"That's what I mean!" exclaimed Lintball. "You've remembered every single one haven't you?"

Steve blushed and nodded his head.

"You'll carry those images with you for life—even into your marriage!"

"But Lintball, how do I put these types of thoughts out of my mind?"

"Stevie, my boy, the Bible gives us some advice here. It says, 'Whatever is true, whatever is noble, whatever is right, whatever is pure, whatever is lovely, whatever is admirable—if anything is excel-

lent or praiseworthy—think about such things'
(Philippians 4:8). So, the first step is to avoid
sexual images whenever
possible. But, if any come to your
mind and you find yourself
thinking about them over
and over, then make a decision to replace them with
good thoughts."

"Maybe I could do that by
praying or writing down my
thoughts in a diary or journal?"

"You bet. Or, reading the Bible
or even memorizing Scripture can
also be helpful."

Steve looked thoughtful for a
moment and asked, "Lintball, one last
question. If I do masturbate, even if
it's only once in a while, will God forgive
me?"

"Steve, once again the Bible has the answer. It
says, "If we confess our sins, (God) is faithful and

Get Stronger

There are some won-
derful words of wisdom
in Proverbs 4:20-27.
"Guard your heart, for it
is the wellspring of life."
Even though you are still
young, it is important that you
make wise decisions about all
areas of your life. This
proverb advises you to keep
your eyes straight ahead. He
says to stay on the path and
not to swerve to the right
or to the left as you walk
along life's pathway. Keep
focusing on the kind of man
you want to become and
keep moving toward that
goal. Living God's way is
the safest and best way to
avoid problems that will make
your life difficult later on.

just and will forgive us our sins and purify us from all unrighteousness (1 John 1:9).' God wants a relationship with you for eternity. He wants to guide you and teach you. He wants you to look more and more like his son, Jesus."

"Wow, that's really good to know!" Steve replied. "Thanks!"

"That's what I'm here for, Steve-o!" Lintball Leo replied. "But, one more thing."

"What's that?"

"I love being your friend and advisor, but God has also given two other men to guide and teach you. One is your dad and the other is your pastor or youth pastor. I'd encourage you to talk to them about these kinds of things. Be sure that they are all right with what I'm telling you. OK?"

"Yeah," replied Steve. "I guess it's time for me to spend some time with my dad."

"I'd recommend it, my little friend."

Steve laughed, "Who you calling little?"

He and Lintball both laughed together.

Chapter 10

Why Did God Say "Wait!"?

Lintball Leo was sleeping soundly and snoring loudly. Steve thought it was funny to watch his little fuzzy friend while he slept. He poked Lintball gently. "Hey sleepyhead, are you going to sleep all day?" Steve asked Lintball Leo.

"Walk in
the ways of
good men and
keep to the
paths of the
righteous."
Proverbs 2:20

"What? Who's there? What's going on?" Lintball

Leo said, as he woke up, rubbing his little eyes.

"Oh, good morning Steve, what time is it? Did I

oversleep again?" he asked his friend.

"No, you didn't oversleep, Lintball Leo," Steve

said. "I just woke up early. I had a lot on my mind.

You know—questions keep racing through my

head."

"Yeah I know. Whenever I have something on my

mind, it's tough for me to stay asleep. So what's on your mind, Steve?" Lintball Leo asked.

"Well," Steve said, "what's really bugging me is why my parents are afraid to talk to me about sex."

"Yes. Most parents would rather have a root canal done with no painkiller than talk with their kids about sex. And that's rather sad when you think about it. In my opinion, the fact that most dads are afraid to talk to their boys about sex is one of Satan's greatest victories. Sex is one of the most wonderful gifts that God has designed and given to men and women. Satan knows that. He's glad when dads keep silent on the subject. He figures that boys will get bad information elsewhere and never really understand what God intended when he cre-ated sex."

"I never thought about it that way," Steve said, thoughtfully.

"When a dad hasn't been taught God's view of healthy sex, he often finds it difficult or embarrassing to discuss it with his

son," Lintball went on. "But when a dad understands what the Bible says—how God designed sex and gave it to us as a gift to enjoy and how we can actually honor God and his design by saving sex for marriage—he will be anxious to talk to his son about it. At the right time and place, that is."

Steve laughed.

"What's so funny?" Lintball Leo asked his friend.

"Well, I never really thought about sex being a gift from God," he replied.

"It is," Lintball Leo continued. "If your dad is uncomfortable talking with you about it, you can help by asking him questions about sex. Just like you have been doing with me. It's probably best to ask about this subject at a time when your mom and dad aren't busy," Lintball Leo advised.

"One thing confuses me, Lintball," Steve said. "Sex is God's invention, right?"

"Right."

"And he wants it to be romantic and wonderful and used only when we are married. Right?"

"Right."

"But sometimes it's tough not to fantasize about sex."

"Yes, I know. And you're not alone, Steve," Lintball Leo advised his friend. "*Many* boys are troubled by sexual fantasies. After all, you can't turn on the TV or go to the movies without seeing sexual images.

Sex is one of the most wonderful gifts that God has given to men and women.

But the Bible gives us a clue how to avoid sexual temptation. In 2 Timothy 2:22, it says: *Flee the evil desires of youth, and pursue righteousness, faith, love and peace, along with those who call on the Lord out of a pure heart."*

"Wow, I didn't know the Bible talked about stuff like that," Steve said, "I think I'll start reading it more."

"Because he himself suffered when he was tempted, he is able to help those who are being tempted."
Hebrews 2:18

"Good idea,"

Lintball Leo encouraged his friend. "If you take the Bible's advice to 'flee lust' and really go after the good stuff, Steve, you'll *never* regret your decision! Be careful about what you watch on television, at the movies, and on the computer. Stay away from pornography. It's addictive. And always remember that God designed sex for you to enjoy *when* you're married."

"Yes, I think I'll write 'flee lust' on my bulletin board in my room," Steve announced. "But you

To you!
From God.

know Lintball, I wonder why God gave boys such a big sexual interest if he wants them to wait until they get married."

"I know. It's tough and I'm sure most boys wonder why God planned it that way," Lintball Leo replied. "Your appetite or desire for sex is also something that God created within you. It is not dirty or evil, but a wonderful gift that God designed and placed within you. God created the hormones—especially the one called testosterone—that trigger the brain and make women tantalizing to you. Now I realize you probably aren't actually thinking of having sex yet, but it's coming."

"I never thought about it in those terms," replied Steve.

"Your biggest struggle for the next few years might be controlling your sexual urges. It's tough, but it can be done. God tells men to control this desire. And in the Bible, he says many times that we are to keep ourselves sexually pure. He says we are to save the gift of sex for marriage," Lintball Leo said.

"That sounds like something I should remember!" Steve said with enthusiasm.

Get Smarter

Does it seem to you that your parents say "wait" more than they say "all right, go ahead"?

Sometimes it seems that way with God too. One of the things he wants us to wait for is sex. As you get just a little older, it will seem to you like everyone is doing it. But God said wait until you are married.

God isn't the great spoiler of fun. He knows what is best. After all he made you and he knows becoming involved in sex outside of marriage is going to hurt you and somebody else. Waiting is not only good advice, it's godly.

"Please do, and remember that if God asks you to do something, he will also give you the strength and power to do it." Lintball gave Steve a big fuzzy smile. "And by the way, Steve, it's good to talk to your parents if possible. Remember they were young once and understand a lot of what you are going through. They can be a big help to you."

Chapter 11

It Gets Really Embarrassing

"Hey Steve, where are you? When you put me on

the dresser, I don't know where you are," Lintball

Leo complained, looking all around.

"Are you home?"

Lintball heard the toilet flush and saw

Steve come out of the bathroom.

"I'm here, little buddy.

I was just using

the bathroom."

"That's more information than I needed to know" Lintball Leo teased his friend.

"Well, actually, Lintball, I didn't really have to use the bathroom. I just went in there to change my pajamas. I think I had a wet dream while I was asleep," Steve confessed.

"Now that's *really* more information that I need to know!"

Steve looked sad.

"Steve, I'm just teasing! Lighten up a little, will you?" Lintball Leo said to his friend.

Steve looked relieved. "I just learned about wet dreams in biology class last week. I never thought it would happen to me though—but now it has."

"It happens to the best of guys, Steve, " Lintball Leo reassured his friend. "When boys go through puberty, they experience wet dreams. During the part of sleep in which dreams most commonly occur, boys can have erections and then semen—a

combination of sperm from the testicle and fluid—

forms wet, sticky spots on their underwear or

pajama pants. They may think they've wet their

pants, but they've just had a *wet dream*," said

Lintball Leo.

"That's what our biology teacher said too," Steve

said. "He also told us even if we feel embarrassed

"In the image
of God
has God
made man."
Genesis 9:6

or confused, we should remember that wet dreams are completely normal. It just feels weird, that's all."

"Yes, Steve, the first few times you have a wet dream it does feel pretty weird. But remember that wet dreams can't be controlled voluntarily—in other words, you can't keep them from happening. Almost all guys experience wet dreams during puberty and many grown men have them too," said Lintball Leo.

Steve thought about that for a moment then continued talking with his fuzzy friend. "Hey Lintball, you know what's even more embarrassing than having a wet dream?"

"Well, I can guess," said Lintball Leo. "You're talking about having an erection at the worst possible time—like when the teacher calls on you, and you have to stand up and give your answer to the entire class."

"How did you know what I was talking about?" asked Steve.

Lintball answered, "Hey, I was a little lintball once. I went to school too, you know."

Steve thought about Lintball Leo as an even smaller fuzz ball and smiled.

"Steve, did you know that some boys don't even know what an erection is?" Lintball Leo asked.

"I do. We learned all about erections in health

class," Steve replied. He cleared his throat and spoke like a radio announcer. "Erections are when the penis fills with blood and becomes rigid. Erections are a per-fectly normal function of the male body. And they are especially common in young men who are going through puberty."

Lintball Leo was impressed with his young friend's knowledge. "Tell me more about what you learned in health class, Steve."

"Certainly," Steve said proudly. He put on his radio announcer voice again. "Erections can happen while you're doing something pleasurable or some- thing that causes a strong emotion, like excitement or fear. They can also occur for no reason at all and in the oddest places—like church!"

"Right again!" Lintball Leo said. "Erections of the penis are normal and can occur at any time of the day or night, especially for teenage boys. It does not mean that you're gay or becoming a sex maniac. Having an erection is not sinful, it's just another gift from God!"

"Wow, God sure gave us plenty of gifts, didn't he?" Steve responded to his fuzzy little friend.

"He sure did. He sure did!" Lintball Leo agreed.

"Well, I guess I shouldn't worry about erections and wet dreams so much, should I?" Steve asked Lintball Leo.

"No, don't worry. Erections and wet dreams are all part of growing up, and you shouldn't waste any

Get Deeper

Some of growing up and going through puberty is difficult. Just remember that Jesus was once a boy becoming a man too. He understands everything you are going through and he cares. Nothing is happening to your body that is out of his control or he doesn't know about. He has a perfect plan for you and if you can be patient, you'll see it all in time. For now, just get to know Jesus better by praying and reading your Bible — every day if you can.

time or energy worrying about either one of them.

That's for sure,"

Lintball Leo advised.

"I knew I could count on you for good advice,

Lintball," said Steve. "I'm *really* glad that you're my

friend."

"Back at you, good buddy!" said Lintball Leo as he

and Steve did a high five.

Chapter 12

Moods and Emotions: Inhale-Exhale

"Hey Lintball," Steve said, "have you ever been happy one minute, and then really sad or frustrated the next?

"Yes. Why do you ask?"

Because that's what happens to me sometimes, and I'm wondering if I'm the only one."

Lintball Leo stopped brushing his hair for a moment as he thought about how to answer his young friend. "Hmm," Lintball Leo replied, as he tried in vain to get one piece of hair to stop sticking straight up in the air. He licked his fingers again and tried to slick the wild piece of hair into place. "There! Finally! Now I'm ready to start my day," Lintball Leo said.

"Everyone should be... slow to become angry, for man's anger does not bring about the righteous life that God desires."
James 1:19, 20

Steve was amused as he watched the piece of hair once again slowly rise up and stick out of the top of his fuzzy little friend. "Hey Lintball," Steve said, chuckling, "you better just ignore that piece of hair. You're fighting a losing battle there, you know?"

Lintball Leo sighed and agreed with him. "Yes, you're probably right. There were times when something like a wild piece of hair would drive me crazy. I would get so frustrated, but then I realized how silly it was."

Steve thought about that for a moment. "Yes, it's pretty silly to get upset about something that really doesn't matter that much." Steve said. "But why am I so moody sometimes? And why are there times when I don't want anyone near me? Is all that part of the puberty thing too?"

"Frequent mood changes are part of growing up, *especially* when you're going through puberty," Lintball Leo explained. "They can be bothersome,

but they're a com-
mon problem. Your
mood swings can
create some big
problems for your
parents who wonder
where their nice little

boy went. So if they're a problem for
you, just know they're a real pain for your family,
your friends, and even your teachers."

"Yeah, I know," Steve
said. "Just the other
day this guy in
class was so
moody he was
driving our
teacher a little
crazy."

"Not a good

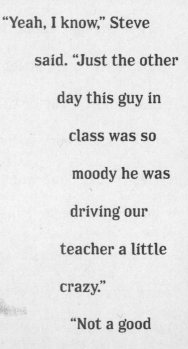

thing to do to your teacher, that's for sure," Lintball Leo said. "Sudden and dramatic mood changes happen because your body is producing a host of hormones in amounts you have never experienced before. Those hormones, especially the male hormone testosterone, are causing changes in your voice and body as well as changes in your mind and emotions."

"Wow!" said Steve. "That explains a lot."

"Before puberty you may have felt happy or sad, calm or angry, stimulated or depressed," Lintball Leo continued. "But during this transition from boyhood to manhood, those emotions may be exaggerated—big time! When you're happy, you can be exceedingly joyful, and when you're sad, you can be incredibly sad. Just remember that these mood swings are normal. They're caused by hormone changes."

"But I shouldn't let my emotions rule my life, should I, Lintball?" Steve asked.

"Wow, how old did you say you are, Steve? That's a good observation and a very good question," Lintball Leo replied in amazement. "The Bible says that when you are filled with the Holy Spirit, the result is love, joy, peace, patience, kindness, good-ness, faithfulness, gentleness, and self-control. If your life does not show these kinds of fruit, then perhaps you're being controlled by your hormones rather than by the Holy Spirit," he continued.

"That's important information to have."

"Yes it is," Lintball Leo replied. "A long time ago, I learned a technique called 'spiritual breathing.' In physical breathing, you exhale—blow out—the bad or impure air. Then, you inhale—breathe in—the good or pure air. The same principle applies for spiritual breathing. As soon as you realize you're doing something wrong, stop and exhale by confessing it to God. Say, 'God, you're right. I'm wrong to be acting this way. I admit it to you and to myself.' You see, Steve, the Bible teaches that when you confess your sins to God, he is faithful and righteous and will forgive your sin and cleanse you from all unrighteousness."

Get Cooler

Moodiness goes along with growing up and having those hormones raging through your body. But who likes to be around someone who is moody all the time? Nobody. Find a way to handle your anger and moodiness that is not destructive to those around you. How about a fast game of basketball or a job around town? How about writing your feelings in a journal and then closing the journal and going back to your family or friends with a smile on your face? How about spending some time talking about how you're feeling — with your dad or youth pastor. They'll appreciate your asking and your life will be calmer.

"I like God," Steve said. "I think he's pretty cool."

"Yes, he's very cool," Lintball Leo said. "But after you've exhaled the wrong out, don't neglect to take the next step. Inhale. Take a spiritual breath by telling God you want to put his Holy Spirit in charge of your life. He'll help you miss some of the bumps of life. He'll help you smooth out your emotions—even when your hormones are raging!"

"That sounds like great advice. Thanks again for

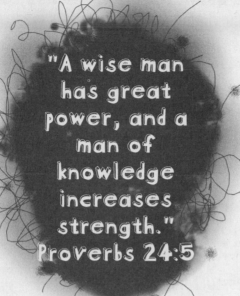

"A wise man has great power, and a man of knowledge increases strength."
Proverbs 24:5

being my friend, Mr. Lintball Leo," Steve said.

Lintball Leo took a bow and replied, "You are most certainly welcome my friend!"

smarter•stronger
2:52
twofiftytwo
deeper•cooler

The 2:52 Boys Bible–
the "ultimate *manual*" for boys!

The 2:52 Boys Bible, NIV
General Editor Rick Osborne

From the metal-looking cover to the cool features inside, *The 2:52 Boys Bible, NIV* is filled with tons of fun and interesting facts–yup, even gross ones, too!–that only a boy could appreciate. Based on Luke 2:52: "And Jesus grew in wisdom and stature, and in favor with God and men," this Bible will help boys ages 8-12 become more like Jesus mentally, physically, spiritually, and socially–Smarter, Stronger, Deeper, and Cooler!

Hardcover 0-310-70320-4
Softcover 0-310-70552-5

Zonder**kidz**.

This great CD holder for young boys has a rubber 2:52 Soul Gear™ logo patch stitched onto cool nylon material. This cover will look great with the newly released 2:52 Soul Gear™ products. The interior has 12 sleeves to hold 24 favorite CDs.

$9.99 ($15.50 Cdn)

ISBN: 0-310-99033-5
UPC: 025986990336

This cool book and Bible Cover for young boys will look great with the newly released 2:52 Soul Gear™ products. It features a rubber 2:52 logo patch stitched down onto microfiber material. The zipper pull is black with 2:52 embroidered in gray. The interior has pen/pencil holders.

$14.99 ($22.50 Cdn) each

Large   ISBN: 0-310-98824-1
        UPC: 025986988241
Med   ISBN: 0-310-98823-3
        UPC: 025986988234

inspirio
The gift group of Zondervan

We want to hear from you. Please send your comments
about this book to us in care of the address below.
Thank you.

Zonder**kidz**.

Grand Rapids, MI 49530
www.zonderkidz.com